W9-ABY-993

NAT TURNER AND THE
VIRGINIA SLAVE REVOLT

By Rivvy Neshama

The Child's World®

GRAPHIC DESIGN
Robert E. Bonaker / Graphic Design & Consulting Co.

PROJECT COORDINATOR
James R. Rothaus / James R. Rothaus & Associates

EDITORIAL DIRECTION
Elizabeth Sirimarco Budd

COVER PHOTO
©Nathan Benn/CORBIS

Library of Congress Cataloging-in-Publication Data
Neshama, Rivvy.
Nat Turner and the Virginia slave revolt / by Rivvy Neshama.
p. cm.
Includes index.
Summary: Examines the life of Nat Turner and the events
leading up to the slave rebellion he led in 1831.
ISBN 1-56766-744-9 (lib. reinforced : alk. paper)

1. Turner, Nat, 1800?–1831 — Juvenile literature.
2. Southampton Insurrection, 1831 — Juvenile literature.
3. Slaves — Virginia — Southampton County — Biography —
Juvenile literature. 4. Slave insurrections — Virginia —
Southampton County — History — 19th century — Juvenile
literature. 5. Southampton County (Va.) — History — 19th
century — Juvenile literature. [1. Turner, Nat, 1800?–1831.
2. Slaves. 3. Afro-Americans — Biography. 4. Southampton
Insurrection, 1831.] I. Title.

F232.S7 N47 2000   00-021399
975.5'552 — dc21

Contents

Born a Slave

This is a story of darkness and light. It tells of a dark, dark time in the history of America. It tells of a time of slavery. It also tells about one man who saw a light in the darkness. What he did helped other people see that light, too. This man's name was Nat Turner. He died for freedom. He was born a slave.

What does slavery mean? It means that people can own other human beings. Slaves are their property, just like a house or horse. Slave owners can make their slaves do whatever they want. And they never have to pay them for their work. Many slaves in America lived their whole lives working for their owners.

Nat Turner was born on October 2, 1800. He was the "property of Benjamin Turner." Because his mother was a slave, Nat was one, too. Like all slaves, he was given the last name of his owner. Benjamin Turner was his master, his **slave master.**

Nat's mother, Nancy, was born free in Africa. Slave traders stole her from her home when she was just a teenager. They took her to Southampton, Virginia, and sold her to Benjamin Turner.

Nat's mother's real name was not Nancy. Nancy was her slave name. Slaves weren't allowed to use their African names or to speak their African languages. Their masters hoped they would forget their homeland and accept their lives as slaves. Nancy never forgot Africa or what it was like to be free.

SLAVERY BEGAN THOUSANDS OF YEARS AGO, AND IT TOOK PLACE IN MANY DIFFERENT COUNTRIES. SLAVERY BEGAN IN AMERICA IN THE 1600S. EUROPEAN SLAVE TRADERS CAPTURED MILLIONS OF AFRICAN PEOPLE. SOMETIMES THE TRADERS PAID OTHER AFRICANS TO HELP THEM. THEY PUT THE PEOPLE THEY CAUGHT IN CHAINS AND TOOK THEM TO AMERICA ON SHIPS.

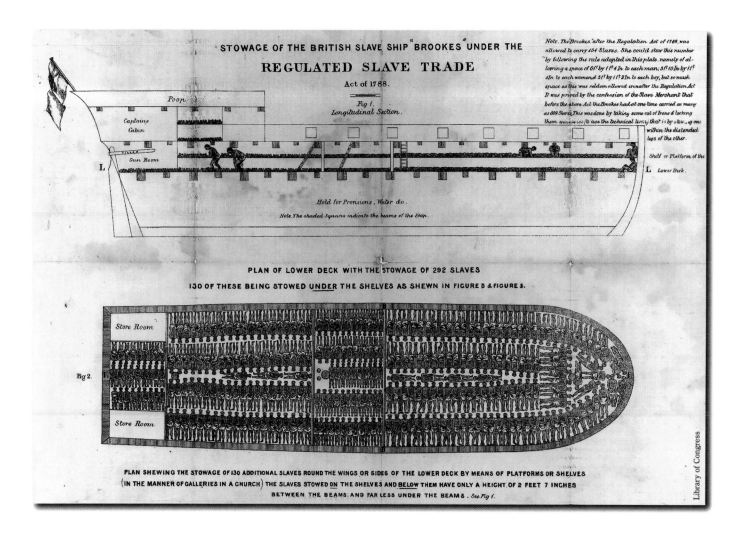

AFRICANS LIKE NAT TURNER'S MOTHER WERE CROWDED ONTO SHIPS AND TAKEN THOUSANDS OF MILES ACROSS THE OCEAN TO AMERICA. THE SLAVE SHIP ABOVE CARRIED 454 PEOPLE. EACH PERSON WAS CHAINED TO A SPOT THAT WAS JUST 16 INCHES WIDE. NO ONE COULD MOVE OR STRETCH. THE JOURNEY ACROSS THE SEA WAS TORTURE.

Nancy loved Nat very much. She taught him to love Africa and to be as hungry for freedom as she was. She also taught Nat to hate slavery. That wasn't hard to do. Anyone would hate being a slave.

Slave children like Nat started working when they were only seven years old. They had to clean the yards and work in the kitchen. By the time they were 12, they were working in the fields. They picked crops and took care of the animals all day long.

Slave children had very little food. They were often hungry. They had hardly any clothes to keep warm. They often had no shoes to wear. At night, they went home to tiny cabins. Many people lived together in these dark, one-room shelters. The cabins had no windows. The floors were made of dirt. The rooms were cold and damp in the winter. Rain leaked through the roofs. Wind blew through cracks in the walls.

THIS DRAWING SHOWS A WOMAN WHO KILLED HER SON SO HE WOULD NOT HAVE TO LIVE A LIFE OF SLAVERY. PEOPLE SAID THAT NAT'S MOTHER HATED SLAVERY SO MUCH, SHE WANTED TO KILL HER SON WHEN HE WAS BORN. SHE THOUGHT IT WOULD BE BETTER FOR HIM TO DIE THAN TO LIVE AS A SLAVE.

Culver Pictures

Most slave masters lived in big, warm houses. Nat's owners, the Turners, were not rich. They often worked with their slaves in the fields. But while Benjamin Turner earned money growing and selling his crops, the slaves only got more tired.

Perhaps the worst part of being a slave was that black people were told they were inferior — not as good or as smart as white people.

The terrible way they were treated made them feel inferior, too. African American slaves had no **rights** and no power. Their owners could control them.

Nat Turner was born in a dark time of fear. Slaves feared cruel masters who could beat them or even kill them without being punished. The slave masters were scared, too. They feared that their slaves would take over or kill them. Those people who wanted slavery to continue said, "Don't worry. That will never happen." They made white people believe that black people were happy being slaves and were too meek to fight for their freedom. Young Nat knew that these things were not true. Someday, he would prove it.

©CORBIS

WHILE THEIR MASTERS LIVED IN LUXURIOUS HOMES, SLAVE FAMILIES LIVED IN SMALL CABINS MADE OF WOOD OR BRICK. MANY FAMILIES WERE TOO LARGE FOR SUCH SMALL LIVING SPACES.

Culver Pictures

MOST SLAVES WORKED ON BIG FARMS, CALLED PLANTATIONS, IN THE SOUTH. PLANTATION OWNERS GREW CROPS OF COTTON, SUGAR, AND TOBACCO. RAISING THESE CROPS TOOK LOTS OF HARD WORK. MANY PLANTATION OWNERS DIDN'T HAVE ENOUGH MONEY TO PAY A LOT OF WORKERS. OTHERS SIMPLY WANTED TO MAKE AS MUCH MONEY AS THEY COULD. TO THE OWNERS, SLAVERY SEEMED LIKE THE PERFECT ANSWER. SLAVES DID ALL THE HARD WORK FOR NO PAY AT ALL.

Anuj Shrestha

NOBODY KNOWS EXACTLY WHAT NAT TURNER
LOOKED LIKE. WHAT PEOPLE DO KNOW IS
THAT HE WAS ABOUT FIVE FOOT, SIX INCHES
TALL. HE WAS A LITTLE BIT STOUT AND HAD
A ROUND FACE.

To Do Great Things

When Nat was born, his parents saw that he had certain **birthmarks** on his head and chest. In Africa, those marks meant that the child was born for a special reason. He was here to help make something great happen. Nat's parents told him this many times as he was growing up.

When Nat was about four years old, something strange happened. He was playing with other children and told them a story. His mother heard him and was very surprised. The story Nat told had happened before he was born! How could he know it? The other slaves were also amazed. They told him that he would grow up to be a **prophet.** They believed he would be a religious leader. They believed that God would speak to him and tell him what to do. Nat never forgot this event and what the people said.

There were other things about young Nat that made him seem special. He was one of the smartest children anyone had ever seen. Masters did not allow their slaves to learn to read or write. Still, some slaves learned to read in secret. Nat was one of them. At that time, even many white people could not read. Nat learned to read when he was very young. Some people say his family taught him, but others say it was his owners. Benjamin Turner was not as cruel as most slave owners. He always allowed Nat to read. Nat loved to read and find out all he could. He learned from everything and everyone.

Culver Pictures

MOST MASTERS DID NOT ALLOW THEIR SLAVES TO LEARN TO READ.
SOMETIMES SLAVES WERE ALLOWED TO LISTEN AS THE MASTER'S
FAMILY READ THE BIBLE ALOUD TO THEM.

Nat's family taught him about the greatness of Africa and the history of his people. Most African American slaves had forgotten about the land of their **ancestors.** Nat never did. He knew where he came from. He knew he was part of a brave and great people.

Nat was very close to his grandmother, Bridget. She was his father's mother, and she was very religious. Nat and Bridget would read the Bible together, over and over. They read about a time when the Jews were slaves in Egypt. They read that God sent his prophet Moses to lead the Jews to freedom. Nat liked to study religion more than anything else.

When Nat was eight or nine, he learned another important lesson. His father ran away from the plantation. Nat knew that other slaves in the South tried to escape. They tried to get to the states in the North. In the North, many white people believed that slavery was wrong and that it should end. Still, most runaway slaves were caught. Then they were punished — or even killed. Nat never knew whether his father found freedom. But his father had left him a valuable gift. He showed Nat that the two most important things in life are to be brave and to be free.

THIS POSTER OFFERED A REWARD FOR A RUNAWAY SLAVE. NAT WORRIED WHEN HIS FATHER RAN AWAY. HE KNEW THAT SLAVES WHO DID SO WERE OFTEN CAUGHT AND SEVERELY PUNISHED. BUT NAT ALSO UNDERSTOOD THAT FREEDOM WAS WORTH FIGHTING FOR.

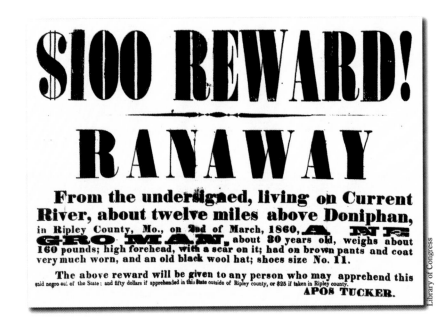

$100 REWARD!

RANAWAY

From the undersigned, living on Current River, about twelve miles above Doniphan, in Ripley County, Mo., on 2nd of March, 1860, A NE GRO MAN, about 30 years old, weighs about 160 pounds; high forehead, with a scar on it; had on brown pants and coat very much worn, and an old black wool hat; shoes size No. 11.

The above reward will be given to any person who may apprehend this said negro out of the State; and fifty dollars if apprehended in this State outside of Ripley county, or $25 if taken in Ripley county.

APOS TUCKER.

FOR MOST SLAVES, THE ONLY HAPPY TIMES WERE SUNDAYS AND CHRISTMAS, WHEN ALL THE SLAVES GOT TOGETHER LIKE A BIG FAMILY. WHEN HE WAS YOUNG, NAT WOULD PLAY WITH THE OTHER CHILDREN. AS HE GREW OLDER, HE TOLD STORIES AND LISTENED TO MUSIC PLAYED ON BANJOS AND FIDDLES. THE SLAVES SANG SONGS THAT TOLD OF THEIR SADNESS AND THEIR HOPES TO BE FREE. NAT HEARD THESE "SORROW SONGS" AND SANG ALONG.

As Nat grew older, he learned more and more. While he worked in the fields, he was always thinking or praying. After work, he would read and do experiments. He taught himself to make paper, pottery, gunpowder, and metal.

Other slaves began to ask Nat for advice and help. They looked up to him and felt he was different. Nat also felt he was different. So he began to spend a lot of time alone. He would pray for many hours. He would also fast, which meant he ate nothing for a long period of time. Fasting was a way for him to feel closer to God.

One day, when Nat was about 20 years old, he was working in the fields and praying. Suddenly, he heard a voice inside his head. The voice spoke words from the Bible. It said, "Seek ye the kingdom of heaven and all things shall be added unto you." Nat believed he was hearing the voice of the **spirit** that spoke to the prophets in the Bible. He had read many times about the spirit talking to Moses. Now he believed that it was talking to him.

Nat was amazed. For two years, he prayed all the time, even as he worked and rested. Again, he heard the voice and the same words. Nat remembered what he had been told as a child. People had said he was born to do great things. The voice he heard made him believe that this was true. He still did not know just what he was born to do. He would have to wait to find out.

The Preacher and the Prophet

When Nat was in his early 20s, many changes came into his life. His first master, Benjamin Turner, had died. His new master was Benjamin's son, Samuel. Times were hard for Virginia farmers. They could not earn much money selling their crops. Some sold their slaves to make money. Others hired **overseers** to make the slaves work even harder.

Overseers were often cruel men who would beat the slaves if they rested at all. Samuel Turner hired an overseer. Right after that, Nat ran away and hid in the woods. No one caught him. Then, after 30 days, he came back on his own.

The other slaves couldn't believe their eyes. Why did Nat come back? Didn't he want to be free? Nat explained to them that he had heard the spirit in the woods. The spirit told him to return.

It reminded him to think of the kingdom of heaven. Some people believe that Nat returned because he was beginning to know what he was there to do. He was not meant to free only himself. He was meant to help free his people.

Soon after Nat returned, he had a vision. A vision is a dream that people have when they are awake. In Nat's vision, he saw white spirits fighting with black spirits. The sun turned dark, and there was a stream of blood. Nat heard a voice tell him that this was what he would see in his life. It said that no matter how hard this would be, it was up to Nat to live through it.

©CORBIS

When Samuel Turner hired an overseer, Nat worried that life on the plantation would become even worse. Overseers were known to treat slaves cruelly, often punishing them harshly with beatings. Nat decided to run away.

Nat spent more time alone than ever. He prayed and he fasted. He wanted to make himself ready for whatever he was called to do. Before that happened, Nat had to face one of the saddest and most terrible things about slavery. Nat had a wife named Cherry, and they had a son. In 1822, Samuel Turner died. All his property was sold. A price was put on every piece of furniture, on every farm animal, and on every slave. Nat and his family were sold to different slave owners. Slave families were often separated this way. Nat was luckier than most. Cherry and his son lived on a farm near his. Sometimes he could see them.

Nat had more and more visions, which he shared with other slaves. Soon he became a **preacher** to his people. Sometimes he preached at secret meetings in the woods. At other times, he preached at black churches on different plantations in Southampton. This way, he learned all the secret paths in his neighborhood. He also learned which slaves he could trust.

People said that Nat was a gentle, quiet man. When he preached, however, he was loud and powerful. He told of the visions he saw and the voice that he heard. He told about the battle between the white and black spirits, and the sun growing dark. He told about **Judgment Day.** The Bible said that on this day, bad people would be punished, and good people would be rewarded. The slaves believed that this meant their masters would finally be punished, and the slaves would be free.

Nat's voice rang strong as he told them that Judgment Day was coming! He was preparing his people for something important. He was preparing them to join him once his plans were made.

Many African Americans saw Nat as their leader. They knew he never drank, smoked, or swore. Some people believed that God spoke to Nat. They called Nat "The Prophet." Nat was a small man. But when people looked at Nat, they saw power and greatness. These things have nothing to do with size.

Culver Pictures

SOME MASTERS TRIED TO KEEP THEIR SLAVES FROM GETTING TOGETHER AT RELIGIOUS SERVICES. EVEN SO, SLAVES GATHERED WHEN THEY COULD TO LISTEN TO A LEADER SPEAK ABOUT GOD AND FAITH. LISTENING TO PREACHERS TELL STORIES AND READ THE BIBLE GAVE THEM HOPE.

In May of 1828, Nat heard another voice. It told him it would soon be time to kill his enemies with their own weapons. Nat finally knew what he had been born to do. Like Moses, he would help free his people from slavery. He would lead the terrible battle he had seen in his vision. Unfortunatly, Nat could think of no way to help his people except through violence. This meant that too many people would be injured or die. In the end, violence would not accomplish Nat's goal. He would not be able to free his people with weapons. Still, he listened to the voice. Nat was patient. He waited.

Three years later, on a sunny day in February 1831, strange things happened in the sky. The sun grew darker and darker, until there was no light left at all. Suddenly, the sky was as dark as night. It was a total **eclipse** of the sun. Some people looked up and thought that the world was ending. Nat looked up and watched the sun darken — just as it had in his vision. The sign he had waited for was here! Nat called a meeting with the four men he trusted most: Henry Porter, Hark Travis, Nelson Williams, and Sam Francis.

They made plans for their **revolt.** It would take place on July 4th. On America's holiday of **independence,** America's slaves would fight for their own independence.

When July 4th came, Nat felt too sick with worry to begin the revolt. He knew that two other big slave rebellions had failed before they even began. Some slave **traitors** had told the slave owners of the plans. The men who planned to lead the revolt were were killed by hanging. New laws were passed that made the lives of slaves even harder. Nat knew all this. He knew that the revolt could mean death for many people. He also knew that he might die. He was only 30 years old.

On August 13, Nat saw another sign in the heavens. Again, the sky grew dark and the sun turned a strange color. This time, Nat was ready to act. He told his four men to meet him in secret that Sunday, August 21.

The man who was called "The Preacher" and "The Prophet" was about to become a **general.**

Anuj Shestha

WHEN NAT SAW THE ECLIPSE OF THE SUN
IN FEBRUARY OF 1831, HE KNEW IT WAS
A SIGN. NOW WAS THE TIME TO ORGANIZE
A REVOLT. HE AND OTHER SLAVES WOULD
FIGHT FOR THEIR FREEDOM.

General Nat's War

On August 21, two other slaves joined Nat and his four men at their meeting in the woods. Their names were Jack Reese and Will Francis. Will had scars all over his body from beatings. Nat asked him why he had come. Will answered, "My life is worth no more than the others, and my **liberty** is dear to me."

This strong wish for freedom was the most powerful weapon these men had. The slave owners had all the money, horses, gunpowder, and guns. Nat's six men had only a hatchet, an ax — and each other. They made plans to start the battle after midnight.

And so the rebellion began. Nat's men moved quietly and secretly in the dark. First they went to the Travis plantation. Nat was working as a slave for Joseph Travis at that time. They killed Joseph Travis and his whole family. No one could be left alive to warn the other slave owners.

The seven rebels took four guns and some gunpowder from the Travis house. Then Nat made his men line up and march with their new guns. He made them see that they were soldiers, not criminals. They were fighting in a war against slavery. They were fighting for freedom.

Nat's soldiers moved quickly from plantation to plantation. At each farm, they killed the slave owner and his family. Then they took all the guns, food, and horses they could find. They also asked all the slaves at each plantation to join them in the fight. Many slaves were too scared. They knew they could be caught and hanged. Still, Nat's army grew bigger and bigger. They rode from farm to farm throughout the night. They killed more than 55 people. No matter how terrible slavery was, what Nat and his soldiers did was wrong. No one has the right to take away the life of another human being. But slavery made these men so angry, they no longer cared about right and wrong.

Library of Congress

NAT GATHERED IN THE WOODS WITH A GROUP OF OTHER SLAVES TO PLAN THEIR REVOLT. ON AUGUST 22, 1831, THE SLAVES BEGAN THE REBELLION AT THE TRAVIS PLANTATION.

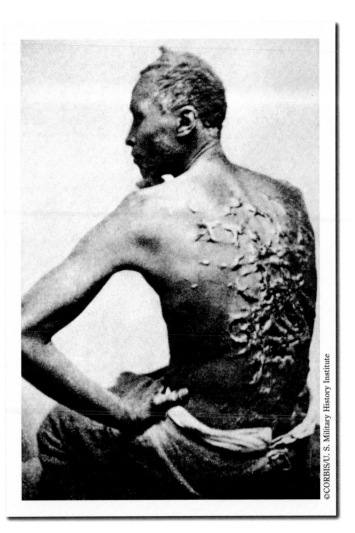

©CORBIS/U. S. Military History Institute

WILL FRANCIS HAD SCARS ALL OVER HIS BODY, MUCH LIKE THIS FORMER SLAVE. WHEN HE JOINED FORCES WITH NAT TO REVOLT AGAINST THEIR MASTERS, WILL SAID HE WASN'T AFRAID. NAT ASKED HIM IF HE THOUGHT HE WOULD GAIN HIS FREEDOM. WILL SAID, "I WILL, OR LOSE MY LIFE."

It was a dark and violent night of blood, fear, and tears. It was a night born from the darkness, pain, and violence of slavery.

By Monday morning, Nat's army had more than 60 soldiers. Most had found guns and were riding on horses. They shouted and cheered when Nat rode toward them. He was their general, and they listened to his orders.

Now, Nat ordered his men to ride to Jerusalem. Jerusalem was the main town in Southampton County. Many guns and lots of gunpowder were stored there. Nat also believed that they would find more slaves to join their army in the town. He knew secret paths that led there.

On their way to Jerusalem, Turner's army met a group of 18 white men. They had guns and were on horses. This was the first real battle in Turner's war. It took place at James Parker's farm. General Nat ordered his men to fire and rush forward. They did — and they won.

There wasn't time to rest, though. Nat's revolt was no longer a secret. Church bells were ringing in Jerusalem to warn people to hide and take arms. Many more white men with guns soon attacked Nat's army. Nat saw some of his bravest men get hurt or killed. Some of his men rode away, hoping to escape. Others had been drinking brandy that they had found at the plantations. They were too drunk to fight well.

Nat could not find enough men to make their way to Jerusalem. So he turned back. He hoped to gather all his men together again later. He was still riding with about 40 of his soldiers. They saw white men with guns wherever they went. They knew that these guns were much more powerful then theirs were. Many of Nat's soldiers were just teenagers, and they had never been taught to fight. There were more shootings, and more of Nat's men ran away. Nat believed that many men had been caught and made to betray him. After two days, Nat returned to the Travis plantation. There, he dug a cave and hid.

Library of Congress

TURNER'S REVOLT LASTED ALMOST THREE DAYS. BY THE TIME IT WAS OVER, TURNER AND HIS MEN HAD KILLED **57** PEOPLE.

By now there were 3,000 white men with guns marching from Virginia and other states to Southampton. Many white people were scared and angry. They wanted **revenge.** Nat's army had used violence as a way to scare the slave owners. The revolt had been more violent than any other slave uprising before it. They wanted the slave masters to be too scared to fight back. Nat wanted them to give up and free the slaves. Now, the white army used violence to scare the slaves. They wanted them to be too scared to rebel ever again. So they killed more than 100 African Americans. They beat and punished many more.

So much death. So much sadness. All of it happened because of slavery. When something wrong is allowed to exist, it makes other bad things happen. Slavery was very wrong.

The rebels of Nat's army were caught and put in jail. Many were hanged. But where was General Nat? People all over Virginia were scared that he would fight again. Men with dogs were searching for him. They didn't know he was hiding in a dark hole. At night, Nat would sneak out to find water and food. Then he would hide again.

Maybe he was thinking about the battle he had lost. Maybe he was also thinking about what he had won. General Nat had led the biggest slave revolt in U.S. history. He had put together an army of African Americans to fight for freedom. Even his men who died had died free.

Most black people knew this. They loved Nat and saw him as a hero. They believed he had the right to rebel. They were proud of his courage.

Most slave owners hated and feared Nat. Until they found him, they would be afraid to sleep. While they looked for Nat Turner, they shot more and more slaves.

Darkness and Light

After hiding for six weeks, Nat was caught on October 30 by a man with a shotgun. The man's name was Benjamin Phipps. Nat was taken to a jail in Jerusalem. The judge asked him to admit that what he had done was wrong. Nat said no. He knew that what was really wrong was slavery. He believed that what he did was necessary to make slavery end.

A white lawyer named Thomas Gray visited Nat in jail. He found Nat to be a man of great intelligence. Nat told him the story of his life and his revolt. Gray later published Nat's story and called it *The Confessions of Nat Turner*.

In his "confessions," Nat said that the reasons for his revolt began with his birth. Although he was born a slave, he had been born for great things. Nat also told Gray about the voices he heard and the visions he saw. He explained how his revolt was a religious battle. He believed he had done what the spirit wanted him to do.

Nat's beliefs made Gray and some other people call him a religious **fanatic.** They thought he was too religious to see things clearly. They also saw him as a violent man who was full of anger. Yet the black and white people with whom Nat grew up always said he was a gentle man. Perhaps he was a gentle man who felt the anger and rage of all his people — a people who had been enslaved for more than 200 years.

©CORBIS

MOST OF NAT'S SOLDIERS WERE CAUGHT RIGHT AWAY, BUT HE
WAS ABLE TO HIDE IN THE WOODS FOR SIX WEEKS. A REWARD OF
$1,100 WAS OFFERED FOR HIS CAPTURE. EVENTUALLY, A MAN
NAMED BENJAMIN PHIPPS CAUGHT HIM.

THE
CONFESSIONS
OF
NAT TURNER,
THE LEADER
OF
THE LATE INSURRECTION
IN SOUTHAMPTON, VA.

AS FULLY AND VOLUNTARILY MADE TO

THOMAS R. GRAY,

In the prison where he was confined, and acknowledged by him to be such,
when read before the Court of Southampton: with the
certificate, under seal of the Court convened at
Jerusalem, Nov. 5, 1831, for his trial.

ALSO,

AN AUTHENTIC ACCOUNT

OF THE

WHOLE INSURRECTION,

WITH

Lists of the Whites who were Murdered,

AND OF THE

Negroes brought before the Court of Southampton,
and there sentenced, &c.

RICHMOND:
PUBLISHED BY THOMAS R. GRAY.

T. W. WHITE, PRINTER.

1832.

A WHITE LAWYER NAMED THOMAS R.
GRAY INTERVIEWED NAT TURNER. THE
INTERVIEW WAS READ IN COURT AND
THEN PUBLISHED IN A BOOK CALLED
THE CONFESSIONS OF NAT TURNER.

Nat's **trial** was held on November 5. He was accused of planning and leading a revolt. Nat had already admitted to all he had done. Still, he said he was not guilty. That's because he did not believe that what he did was wrong. The judge did not agree. He said that Nat was guilty and would be killed by hanging.

On November 11, 1831, Nat Turner walked to the hanging tree. He looked brave and calm. His faith was as strong as ever. His only words before he died were, "I am ready."

Some slaves remembered how Nat had said that there would be rain and darkness after he died. It did rain, and it did turn dark — for Nat's people. It was a dark time because many African American slaves were treated worse than before. Some were even killed. Most of them were innocent and had nothing to do with the revolt. It was also dark because new laws were passed that made the lives of slaves even harder. They could no longer meet for prayer by themselves. Instead, a white person always had to be with them. The new laws said that no African American could be a preacher. They said that anyone who taught a slave to read or write would be severely punished.

Yet even in this darkness, a light was growing brighter. It was the light of truth. After Nat Turner's revolt, white people no longer said that African Americans were content to be slaves. They no longer said that black slaves would never rebel. They began to see that no one can keep other people as slaves. For no matter how hard people try, the human spirit cannot be enslaved or held down. Someday, it will rise up and fight for freedom.

There was also the light of **inspiration.** What Nat did inspired and led more people — whites and blacks — to speak out against slavery. Most of these people lived in the North. They were called **abolitionists.** They wanted to abolish, or end, slavery. Nat's actions and bravery also inspired future African Americans to continue the fight for freedom. His revolt proved that African Americans would die to end slavery.

Another shining light was the light of hope. For more than 200 years, African American slaves never gave up hope. Nat Turner made their hope grow stronger. After General Nat's revolt, there was real hope that slavery would end one day.

That day came in 1865, after the long **Civil War.** For four years, African American soldiers joined white soldiers from the North in fighting against the South and against slavery. Finally, the North won the war. The government soon passed new laws to outlaw slavery in the United States forever.

At last, there was the light of freedom. This was the light Nat Turner saw in the darkness: the chance for freedom. He gave his life to make that light grow brighter. Now, everyone else could see it, too.

Library of Congress

THIS IS THE TREE WHERE NAT TURNER WAS HANGED ON NOVEMBER 11, 1831. TURNER'S REVOLT WAS IMPORTANT BECAUSE IT PROVED THAT AFRICAN AMERICANS WERE WILLING TO FIGHT — AND EVEN DIE — FOR THEIR FREEDOM.

Library of Congress

An artist drew this sketch of Nat Turner based on people's descriptions of him. Although Nat confessed to all he had done, he still said he wasn't guilty of a crime. He believed the evil of slavery forced him to revolt.

Timeline

1600s Slavery begins in America.

1800 Nat Turner is born in Southampton, Virginia, on October 2. He is born a slave of Benjamin Turner's.

1820 Nat hears a spirit telling him what to do and speaking words from the Bible.

1821 Nat runs away from the farm of Samuel Turner and then comes back on his own.

Nat marries a slave named Cherry, and they have a son.

Nat has a vision of black and white spirits fighting. In his vision, he also sees the sun turning dark.

1822 Samuel Turner dies. Nat and Cherry are sold to different slave owners.

1825 Nat becomes a preacher.

1828 Nat hears a voice telling him it will soon be time to kill his enemies. The voice says to wait for a sign in the heavens.

1831 A major eclipse of the sun occurs in February. Nat believes this is the sign for which he was waiting.

On August 13, Nat sees another sign in the heavens. Again, the sky grows dark, and the sun turns a strange color.

On August 22, Nat and his men begin the slave revolt. It lasts for a few days before state and federal troops stop it. Nat hides for nearly six weeks before he is captured on October 30 and taken to jail.

Nat tells his "confessions" to lawyer Thomas R. Gray on November 1. Four days later, Nat goes to trial and is found guilty of planning and leading a slave revolt.

Nat is hanged in Jerusalem, Virginia, on November 11. He is 31 years old.

1865 The American Civil War ends in April. Slavery is officially ended by the 13th Amendment to the Constitution at the end of the year.

Glossary

abolitionists
(ab-uh-LISH-uh-nists)
Abolitionists were people who worked to end (abolish) slavery. Nat Turner inspired many abolitionists.

ancestors
(AN-ses-terz)
Ancestors are someone's family's members who were born long before, such as grandparents or great grandparents. Nat Turner's ancestors were from Africa.

birthmarks
(BERTH-marks)
Birthmarks are marks on the skin that people have when they are born. People told Nat Turner that his birthmarks meant he was going to do something important in his life.

Civil War
(SIV-ill WAR)
The Civil War in the U.S. was fought between the northern and southern states. The war lasted from 1861 and 1865.

eclipse
(ee-KLIPS)
During an eclipse of the sun, the moon comes between the sun and the Earth. When this happens, the moon blocks part or all of the sun's light, so the Earth's sky grows dark.

fanatic
(fuh-NAT-ik)
A fanatic is someone who always talks or thinks about something they like or believe. Some people called Nat Turner a fanatic because of his strong religious beliefs.

general
(JEN-er-el)
A general is an important army officer who tells soldiers what to do. People called Nat Turner "General Nat."

independence
(in-dee-PEN-dentz)
Independence is freedom. July 4th, known as Independence Day, is the U.S. holiday that celebrates the nation's independence.

inspiration
(in-speh-RAY-shun)
An inspiration is someone or something that encourages a person to do good things. Nat Turner was an inspiration to African Americans.

Judgment Day
(JUDJ-ment DAY)
Some people believe that Judgment Day is a day when all bad people will be punished by God and all good people will be rewarded. Nat Turner told other slaves that Judgment Day was coming, and that slave masters would be punished.

Glossary

liberty
(LIB-er-tee)
Liberty means freedom. General Nat and his soldiers wanted liberty.

overseers
(oh-vur-SEE-urz)
In the time of slavery, an overseer was someone whose job was to make the slaves work very hard, often by being cruel. Nat Turner's owner hired an overseer.

preacher
(PREE-chur)
A preacher is someone who gives a religious talk to people. Preachers often give talks at a church service.

prophet
(PRAH-fit)
A prophet is a person who is believed to speak for God. A prophet can also be someone who tells the future or is a religious leader.

revenge
(REE-venj)
Revenge is doing harm to someone who has harmed you. White people wanted revenge after Nat and his soldiers rebelled.

revolt
(REE-volt)
A revolt is a fight against people in power. Slave owners worried that slaves would start a revolt if they had weapons.

rights
(RYTZ)
Rights are the things that the law says people can have or do, such as the right to vote or to practice religion. African American slaves had few rights.

slave master
(SLAYV MAS-ter)
A slave master was a person who owned slaves. Slave masters could tell slaves what to do and did not have to pay them.

spirit
(SPEER-it)
A spirit is something or someone that cannot be seen, but is heard or felt. Nat believed that a spirit talked to him.

traitors
(TRAY-turz)
Traitors are those who help the enemy of their own people. Slaves who warned the slave owners about rebellions were viewed by the rebels as traitors

trial
(TRY-ul)
A trial is a process used to decide whether a person is guilty or innocent of commiting a crime. Trials take place in a court of law.

Index

Further Information

Books

Bisson, Terry. *Nat Turner, Slave Revolt Leader.* New York: Chelsea House Publishers, 1988.

Kalman, Bobbie. *Life on a Plantation.* New York: Crabtree Publishing Co., 1997.

Kent, Deborah. *African Americans in the Thirteen Colonies.* Danbury, CT: Children's Press, 1996.

Web Sites

Read *The Confessions of Nat Turner* (ask an adult to help you with this difficult text):
http://www.melanet.com/nat/nat.html

Take a quiz about Nat Turner and other well-known African Americans:
http://www.brightmoments.com/blackhistory/fnnat.html

Visit the African American Almanac to play games, read folk tales, and learn about Nat Turner and other African Americans:
http://www.toptags.com/aama/index.htm

Links to information about slavery:
http://www.links2go.com/more/www.melanet.com/nat/